This not

belongs to:

....

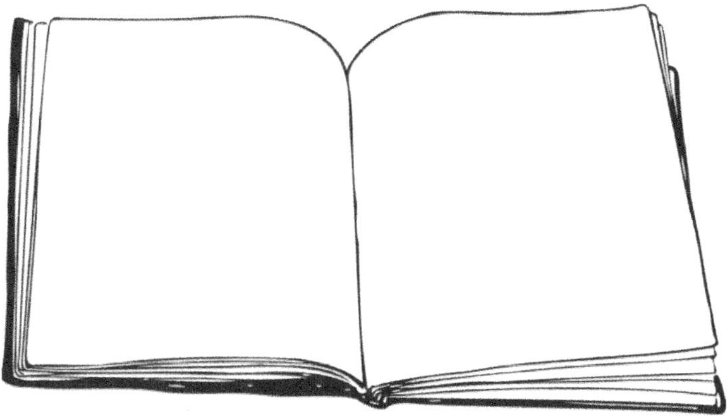

Made in the USA
Monee, IL
09 December 2022

20534260R00070